BEAR HUGS

A GIFT FOR:

_____

FROM:

_____

A true friend is the greatest of all blessings.

Duc De La Rochefoucauld

BEAR HUGS FOR MY FRIEND

Copyright 2002 by Zondervan
ISBN 0-310-98832-2

This edition published by Hallmark Cards, Inc.
under license from Zondervan.

www.hallmark.com

Compiler: Lee Stuart
Associate Editor: Molly Detweiler
Project Manager: Patti Matthews
Design: Mark Veldheer
Photography: Photographic Concepts

Printed in China
05 06 07/HK/9 8 7

BOK4084

BEAR
HUGS

FOR MY FRIEND

GIFT BOOKS
from Hallmark

ZONDERVAN

Friendship is a blessing that
nothing can replace.
It wipes away all my tears
and puts a smile on my face.

Molly Detweiler

Friends are people you make a part of your life because you feel like it. Basically, your friends are not your friends for any particular reason. They are your friends for no particular reason.

Frederick Buechner

In the garden of friendship,

there are annuals and perennials. Some demand careful tending while others flourish with little attention.

Joy MacKenzie

When we bring sunshine
into the lives of others, we're
warmed by it ourselves.

Barbara Johnson

LORD, you
have assigned
me my portion
and my cup;
you have made
my lot secure.

Psalm 16:5

In His plan
for friends, God often
paints way
outside the lines.

Joy MacKenzie

If one falls
down, his friend
can help him up.

Ecclesiastes 4:10

Can't you tell when you're with someone who's listening? She hears you, really hears you.

Sheila Walsh

The best kind of friend is the one you could sit with, hardly saying a word, and then walk away feeling like that was best time you've ever had.

Molly Detweiler

Shoes and skirts
and bracelets,
Earrings and
sweaters too;
The definition
of fun for me
Is a shopping
trip with you!

Carry each other's burdens,
and in this way you will
fulfill the law of Christ.

Galatians 6:2

Bear with each other and forgive whatever grievances you may have against one another.

Colossians 3:13

Giggle potential is everywhere; we just need to slow down long enough to see it.

Marilyn Meberg

If I were asked what I cherish most, my answer would surely be my faith in God, but without so much as a comma between, I would have to add my exquisite treasure of friends.

Peggy Benson

On the road between
the homes of friends,
grass does not grow.

Norwegian proverb

Give, and it will be given to you. A good measure, pressed down, shaken together and running over, will be poured into your lap.

Luke 6:38

A friend is one who
knows all about you and
likes you anyway.

Christi Mary Warner

A cheerful
look
brings
joy to
the heart.

Proverbs 15:30

Studies say that people who have friends live longer and have fewer illnesses, and that a close circle of friends actually helps the immune system work.

Peggy Benson

A friend will go out on a limb for you.

Let us lift up
our hearts and
our hands to
God in heaven.

Lamentations 3:41

A good friend
will never burst
your bubble!

Lee Stuart

I thank my God
every time I
remember you.

Philippians 1:3

A good friend is like
a good dessert—
sweet, not
too rich,
and goes great
with coffee.

Lee Stuart

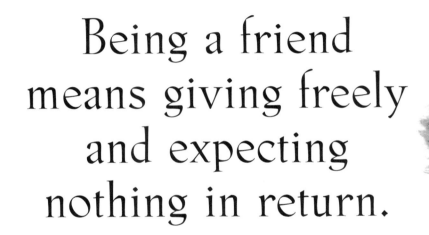

Being a friend means giving freely and expecting nothing in return.

Peggy Benson

If you have much,
give of your wealth;
if you have little,
give of your heart.

A friend loves at all times.

Proverbs 17:17

Some say the best way to forget your troubles is to wear tight shoes, but I say go out and hug somebody.

Barbara Johnson

In all my prayers for…you,
I always pray with joy. It is
right for me to feel this
way about all of you, since
I have you in my heart.

Philippians 1:4, 7

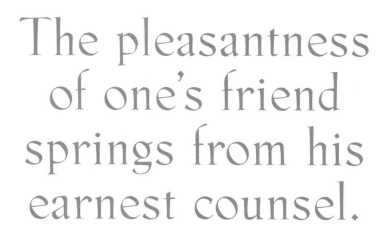

The pleasantness
of one's friend
springs from his
earnest counsel.

Proverbs 27:9

A real friend

is one who walks in when the
rest of the world walks out.

Walter Winchell

Thanks for sharing with me
the riches of your heart!

Oh, the comfort,
the inexpressible
comfort of
feeling safe
with a person.

Dinah Craik

Dear friend, I pray that you may enjoy good health and that all may go well with you.

3 John 1:2

The best mirror is an old friend.

English proverb

You are God's child; you are beautiful,

you are talented; you are a true gift to life.

Sue Buchanan

Friendship is the
breathing rose,
with sweets in
every fold.

Oliver Wendell Holmes

F is for Faithful no matter what
   comes
R is for Relaxing together as
   chums
I is for Inspiration to face each
   new day
E is for Encouragement for
   when skies are gray
N is for Nice to talk with all the
   day long
D is for Devoted to a friendship
   that's strong

SOURCES:

Benson, Peggy, et al., *Friends Through Thick and Thin*, © 1998 by Peggy Benson, et al, (Grand Rapids, MI: Zondervan, 1998).

Johnson, Barbara, *Boomerang Joy*, © 1998 by Barbara Johnson, (Grand Rapids, MI: Zondervan, 1998).

Meberg, Marilyn, et al., *Joy Breaks*, © 1997 by Marilyn Meberg et al, (Grand Rapids, MI: Zondervan, 1997).

Ohrbach, Barbara Milo, *A Token of Friendship*. © 1987 by Barbara Milo Ohrbach. (Clarkson N. Potter, Inc: New York, 1987).

Rikkers, Doris, compiler, *God Made Us Just the Way We Are*, © 2000 by Zondervan, (Grand Rapids, MI: Zondervan, 2000). *God Always Has a Plan B*, © 1999 by Zondervan, (Grand Rapids, MI: Zondervan, 1999).

Warner, Carolyn, *Treasury of Women's Quotations*. © 1992 by Prentice-Hall, Inc. (Englewood Cliffs, NJ: Prentice-Hall, Inc, 1992).